Perth

Photographs
Frances Andrijich

Foreword
Robert Drewe

Text
Jeff Bell

Fremantle Arts Centre Press

Australia's finest small publisher

For Mikhaila, Annaliese, Mary, Gerry and Tricia, with love — Frances.

To Norma and John, my loving and dedicated parents — Jeff.

Contents

Growing up in
the sun

Robert Drewe

Whenever I consider the notion of *home town* — not the place where I happen to live now, or even the city where I've spent the greater part of my life, but where I *come from* — I have a vivid memory of a particular day during my first summer in Perth.

Nothing spectacular happened on this February Sunday and it might not have stuck in my mind if the way of life, the landscape and the weather hadn't still been new to me. In the late spring, my mother and brother and I had left Melbourne and followed my father across the country to a better job, and the sudden heatwave that rolled across our sandy suburb a few weeks later was a novel experience.

I'd recently turned seven and felt for the first time the disadvantages of being born only two weeks after Christmas Day. Christmas had made my mother homesick and weepy; both my parents were heat-dazed and hardly in the mood for more celebrations. My withering hopes for a birthday party had finally died when the two new friends I'd made in our street disappeared to coastal holiday spots.

The memorable day came five or six weeks later, in February. The new school year had just begun and already my second-grade teacher, the stout and crimson-faced Miss Doris Langridge, detested me. She was sarcastic and short-fused and seemed always on the verge of violence. She had a dowager's hump and her bad posture meant she could easily thrust her face down to child level.

Miss Langridge's weapon of choice was a fifteen-inch, state education department-issue wooden ruler. We were all in awe of Miss Langridge's heavyweight ruler. It was inlaid with little squares of West Australian timbers — jarrah, karri, tuart, marri, wandoo, sheoak — and its leading edge was inset with metal, the better to rule a neat line, and to slam the fingers of any boy holding his pen at the wrong angle.

The first day she'd mocked me in front of the class for wearing shoes to school in summer: 'Does Mummy's little darling think he'll get a cold in the tootsies?' The other boys lapped that up. But never mind that they went to school barefoot, my Melbourne mother was adamant: I would not be educated in bare feet. So began the first survival strategy of my life: removing my shoes and socks every morning on the way to school and stuffing them in my schoolbag until I was near home again.

Miss Langridge had won that one: a bitter smirk greeted the sight of my pale naked toes. However her next attack revealed, I see now, at least as much self-loathing as it did a dislike of seven-year-old boys, and me in particular. As her ruler-of-many-local-hardwoods whacked my knuckles once more, this time for not sitting up straight, she yelled, 'You're slumping, Robert Drewe! You must never slump!' And then came the hissing addendum in my face: 'Do you want to end up looking like me?'

Looking like Miss Langridge! The shock of it! That confusing nightmare image, coming on top of her fierce actions, meant that Sundays now mightily depressed me. They had turned into a worrying forerunner to Mondays. All day Sunday I anticipated Monday morning and the savage, over-powdered face of Miss Langridge glowering close to mine, her cheeks quivering with such sudden whipped-up fury that little flakes of dislodged powder floated in the air between us.

The Sunday of which I write was merely another typical summer's day. It was around noon, and I was just home from Sunday school. Waiting for lunch in the hiatus between morning and afternoon, my energy and imagination still flattened by the heat and by Mr Hand the Presbyterian Sunday school teacher's earnest interpretation of Jesus's relentless good works, I went outside and flopped down on the grass in the front yard.

Insects hummed in the bushes. In the kitchen, Garner Ted Armstrong, the radio evangelist, was orating as usual. His haranguing American accent swam in my head. Someone switched stations, first to dirgeful organ music, then to a local country-and-western program — a man and a woman yodelling competitively — then back to Garner Ted, then turned off the radio. Monday and Miss Langridge were looming pretty fast.

I stretched out on my back in the thin shade of a Geraldton wax bush. At once I became aware of the grass under me; its name, I already knew, was buffalo. The grass wasn't exactly prickly but I could feel the blunt blades pressing insistently against my bare arms and legs and on the back of my neck and head. I could feel their concentrated buoyancy under my shirt and shorts. I was lying on a buffalo mattress.

Maybe only an unusual small boy pays such attention to grass. But after the fine soft lawns of Melbourne I was impressed by the buffalo grass. It was sturdy. Each broad blade left an indentation on your skin. I liked the independence of the lawn's individual runners too, the way they struck out optimistically into the dry sandy soil, forever seeking new territory. I liked how the matted strands sprang back after you trod on them. But mostly I liked the name. It was sort of tough and western — cowboyish. If a person was suddenly magically turned into grass, I thought, how much better to be buffalo rather than couch or bent.

As I lay spread eagled I felt completely supported. I let myself sink and the grass held me up. Magpies burbled nearby, trilling 'Pop Goes the Weasel' as usual. I closed my eyes against the sunlight and felt its heat on my eyelids, and for the first time — as I recall — became aware of those amoeba shapes, the kaleidoscope of patterns, swimming in my eyes.

Looking back, I think even at that age I was conscious of something out of the ordinary: a meeting of body and spirit and environment. I'm trying to choose the precise word for the sensual reverie I felt — certainly not one in that seven-year-old's vocabulary. *Perfection* comes close. The buffalo under my back, the warmth of the sun, the sky's clarity, the self-satisfied ruckus of the magpies, the aroma of the Sunday roast wafting from the kitchen: this place where we were now living, was — at that moment at least — simply perfect.

I was called in for lunch then. Although I was hungry I was loath to break the spell. I felt hypnotised. I had to will myself to get up off the grass. And with the feeling of regret that accompanied my rousing myself, I had a flash — and I'm pretty sure this is not a sentimental retrospective sensation — that this was a valuable feeling, one worth remembering. For the time being my Sunday mood, the anxious anticipation of Monday and Miss Langridge, had faded away. My whole attitude to life had been transformed.

I've always felt this was my West Australian epiphany. In that drowsy quarter-hour on the buffalo grass I realised that this sandy, windy place with the vivid skies was home. It was where I came from. Ever since, wherever I've happened to be, I've never doubted I was part of it. Perhaps I've never got off the grass.

*

Maybe I'm not alone. If, as I believe, Australians share, in varying degrees, two central myths — the myth of landscape and the myth of character — all *West* Australians are, without question, one hundred per cent inheritors of the myth of landscape. Unlike the people of most other urbanised, suburbanised, 'civilised' nations and states, the spiritual consciousness draws almost totally on the elements and the environment.

As Professor George Seddon, a painstakingly thorough interpreter of Perth's essence to the world beyond the Nullarbor Plain and the Indian Ocean, points out, the idea of themselves these twenty-first century suburbanites carry in their heads — despite massive cultural input from

▲ *In the 1940s and 1950s, shanty villages sprang up all along the metropolitan coast. At Naval Base a few holiday shacks remain — amongst them is Gudday, built by John Nelson (left) and his 'drunken mates' in the mid-1970s. John, partner Sue Rutland, mother Kitty and son David celebrate Christmas. The Naval Base land is leased from the City of Cockburn for about $700 a year and, like other occupants, John may be ordered to vacate with twenty-eight days notice.*

previous page, left *Acrobatic performers since the early 1990s, Bizircus grew up in Fremantle. They have synthesised a characteristic Australian style combining trapeze, juggling, acrobatics, character clowning, unicycling, whip cracking and of course, stiltwalking.*

previous page, right *Sunrise over Perth.*

elsewhere — is still based chiefly on their weather and surroundings. It's an idea that's still colluding with, or reacting against, attitudes to water and fire, drought and storms, wind and rain, trees and rocks, desert and coastline, held by bush stoics in the nineteenth century.

Colluding with or reacting against? Several years ago, a major exhibition at the state art gallery, *Western Australian Art and Artists 1900–1950*, showed most effectively how an isolated, conservative and conventional society had successfully held off pernicious eastern states and overseas influences for half a century.

According to the exhibition's curator, Janda Gooding,

> *West Australian artists painted a landscape of light, prosperity and promise; a rural arcadia. Images of work and industry or the reality of urban experience were rarely produced. West Australian artists painted the 'ideal' landscape they wanted to see, and in so doing averted their gaze from the reality surrounding them. The myth based on the 'spirit' of the land gained ascendancy in the 1900 to 1950 period and exerted influence on the artists and their public. However, the myth still holds force, forming opinion today.*

Immediately there is an interesting dichotomy. The myth of landscape itself divides into two opposing myths: the Beach versus the Bush, or, as I like to think of it, the Shark versus the Dingo. It's this paradox, the sometimes uneasy relationship between people's coastal and country natures, that makes Western Australia an idiosyncratic place.

West Australians are, above all, hedonists, who enjoy their sensual, casual, invariably coastal, pleasures. The great cartoonist Bruce Petty once satirised Perth in a succinct illustration where a tanned couple was holding an apparently deep and meaningful conversation. One line of dialogue went, 'Another nice day then.' The other was: 'Sorry, am I standing in your sun, Ken?'

Unrestricted access to the Indian Ocean and the Swan River is vital to the West Australian lifestyle, and Frances Andrijich and her publishers have accurately pinned down this obsession, not least in the high proportion of littoral photographs chosen — more than one-third feature river or ocean settings. The boat, whether battered fishing dinghy, racing yacht or luxury cruiser, is king — the next essential purchase in Mr and Mrs Suburbia's life after the obligatory motor car — and an obsession which reached its apotheosis when a local 12-metre yacht, *Australia II*, won the America's Cup in 1983.

But West Australians are also sporty spartans, often physically adventurous, who take pleasure in simple, vigorous (often country) activities oblivious to discomfort — flies, wind, swirling sand — and even danger. Perth congratulates itself on having produced more national sporting champions per capita than any other capital. Few urban Australians are more at ease with outdoor and country pursuits.

For that matter, few big cities in the world offer such proximity to both bush and beach. The way Perth has developed, in a long, narrow coastal strip running north and south of the Swan River mouth, means that few people live more than twenty kilometres from the coast. Always you sense that just over that sandhill is the bush; and back over that dune lies the beach.

*

Ah, the beach. How shall I put this? There is an overwhelming reason most West Australians of a certain age regard the beach in a sensual and nostalgic light. It's because they had their first sexual experience there.

For the rest of their lives, therefore, the beach, the coast (and, in particular, Rottnest Island, the centre of Perth's youthful mating rituals) is not only a regular pleasure, a constant balm, but an idée fixe, an obsession that resurfaces at each critical physical and emotional stage — as new lovers, as honeymooners, as annually vacationing parents, and as the retired elderly.

I suppose it's the sensual, coastal side of their natures that delights in Margaret River's wines and olives, and the succulent local dhufish, crayfish and prawns; that savours equally the salty relief of the afternoon Fremantle Doctor and the delicate transitory blossoms of the eucalyptus. And for their need of clean skies and endless horizons, their lauding of local business and sporting success, not to mention their wary arms-length relationship with the arts, what is responsible but their pragmatic country souls?

*

Ironically, the primal settings of Western Australia do lend themselves superbly to poetry. The poets and novelists, if not the painters, have never averted their gaze. D H Lawrence, for one, saw this eighty years ago, even if his European eyes found a 'spirit of place' that evoked metaphysical terror.

In *Kangaroo*, Lawrence's Richard Somers, a thinly disguised portrait of himself, having decided that Europe 'is done for, played out, finished,' emigrates to 'the newest country: young Australia.' At first, Somers' sense of Western Australia is poetic-mystical:

> *The sky was pure, crystal pure and blue … the air was wonderful, new and unbreathed … but the bush … the grey charred bush. It scared him … It was so phantom-like, so ghostly, with its tall pale trees and many dead trees, like corpses partly charred by bush fires, and then the foliage so dark, like grey-green iron. And then it was so deathly still.*

Exploring the bush on Perth's outskirts, alone, Somers, alias Lawrence, has a more alarming, visceral vision that stays with him through the remainder of his Australian adventure:

> *He walked on, had walked a mile or so into the bush, and had just come to a clump of tall, nude, dead trees, shining almost phosphorescent with the moon, when the terror of the bush overcame him … There was a presence. He looked at weird, white, dead trees, and into the hollow distances of the bush. Nothing! Nothing at all … It must be the spirit of the place. Something fully evoked tonight by that unnatural West Australian moon.*

> *Provoked by the moon, the roused spirit of the bush … It was biding its time with a terrible ageless watchfulness, waiting for a far-off end, watching the myriad intruding white men.*

Lawrence seems easily spooked and his Western Australia is miles and years from mine, but I know what he means about the moon. A full moon might be a film director's cliché, but just as I always associate daytime Perth with summer, whenever I think of Perth by night I see a full moon. Whenever I think of this stark, wind-eroded limestone coast that I love, the word *moonscape* comes to mind. And I consider yet again how it took this weird landmass millions of years to make a single lemon-coloured rock, millions of years to break its crust and weather it down, millions of years to build it again.

*

So the two sides of the West Australian character chafe along, like opposing but complementary political parties, each acting and reacting to the forces around it. On one extreme is the outback, the desert, our history — one is tempted to call it the dry, pessimistic, laconic, male side of the national personality. And on the other is the sea: the fertile, seductive, female side, and our future.

Without being too Jungian about this, I reckon the most interesting part of the West Australian psyche is where the male and female sides get together — the coast. For me, only the coast provides that irresistible combination of bush and ocean. Only the beach provokes that special tingling of the senses that also stands for something else. Romantics could call it youth and love — the sweet frisson of memory that can give bodysurfing another meaning entirely.

*

That any Perth child can grow up in the sun, close to a beach, dreamily lying on the buffalo grass amid the carolling of magpies, is no news to us. What we often fail to grasp is how novel this physical freedom is to foreigners.

It can amaze outsiders that ordinary Perth people seem to carry in their collective unconscious an understanding of the winds and tides, or fishes' schooling habits, or the formation of a limestone river cave, or arcane botanical information about a wildflower seen nowhere else in the nation or the world. How can they know this outdoor stuff so instinctively?

In such an open climate, where immigrant children unfold and grow like flannel flowers in the sun, there is still an optimism that one can accomplish anything, take risks without feeling hamstrung by the past or the accepted way of doing things.

Perth's isolation and prosperity have produced an increasingly self-reliant, comfortable and confident people. This is a city that has already produced two Australian prime ministers, that has been the hub of the nation's mineral wealth for more than a century. There is less of a provincial atmosphere than a generation ago; increasingly, Perth looks north towards the vast markets and complementary cultures of Asia. No longer do local politicians and civic boosters promise earnestly to 'put Perth on the map'. The bottom edge of the map is just fine. In fact, there is pride in being positioned at what the northern hemisphere thinks is the end of the earth, in living in 'the world's most isolated city'.

Some of this optimism is illusory, a sort of summer mirage, like the way Rottnest Island, viewed from the mainland, sometimes seems to break up into pieces and drift off with our memories into the wider ocean. But much of it is true enough.

previous page *Wooden jetties, a feature of the Swan River and a magnet for kids and fishermen, are slowly disappearing because of modern safety concerns and cautious local councils.*

◀ *The Cottesloe pylon is all that remains of an ambitious effort to enclose Cottesloe Beach in a shark proof net. Storms in 1936 put paid to the attempt and the project was abandoned. Though it has no significant practical use today, the pylon serves as a landmark for the famous beach.*

thePeople

the People

By international standards, Perth is not a big city. Even by Australian standards. But Perth is a bright, clean and vibrant city. It is the most remote capital in the world, but each year it is visited by almost as many people as the 1.4 million who live here.

In metropolitan Perth today, the Indigenous population is just over 20,000. When the colonists arrived under the governance of Captain James Stirling in 1829, there are thought to have been about 12,000 Nyungars living in the region. The Nyungar people's traditional way of life was based on the seasons. During the wettest, stormiest months the people sheltered in the Darling Scarp. As the weather became warmer they moved to the river wetlands to feed on fish, eggs and nesting waterbirds. In the hot, dry months, people drank from freshwater springs along the coast, and fed on salmon caught in traps at the water's edge. When the weather cooled and winds swung around to the south-west it was time to start moving to the Scarp again.

Stirling chose the site for Perth because of the seemingly plentiful water supply and the vantage point Mt Eliza provided over potentially hostile navies — the first European exploration had been by the Dutch in the early seventeenth century, followed by the French. The British decided that establishing a colony would thwart France's perceived territorial ambitions.

Unfortunately, the glowing reports made by Stirling were not realised by the early settlers, who found on their arrival that they were in no paradise. It was not until the importation of convict labour in the 1850s and the gold rushes in the 1890s that the colony began to make major progress. By 1901, the state's population had grown to 184,000 and Perth was on the threshold of decades of a booming economy.

In the years following World War Two, a new tide of immigration from the United Kingdom and Europe swelled the population. With an abundance of agricultural resources, and the unlocking of vast mineral wealth in the north and east of the state, there was opportunity for all. The flow of immigrants has continued in the sixty years since the war, although now they are as likely to hail from east and south-east Asia as from Europe. Currently, nearly 29 per cent of all West Australians were born overseas. With this varied cultural background and a local population that loves to travel around the globe, there is little wonder that Perth people are affable hosts to the ever passing parade of tourists and to the migrants who come to settle from all over the world.

previous page, left Interior, Subiaco Hotel.

previous page, right Robert Juniper cruises around Darlington in a Rolls Royce with his wife Patricia and his two dogs (which have ripped the upholstery), is a State Living Treasure and one of Australia's pre-eminent artists. 'I would like to be remembered as an ordinary bloke who left a legacy of paintings for Western Australia,' he says when pushed for a statement. Pictured at Gomboc Gallery with a self-portrait soon after a stroke in January 2002 which immobilised his left arm, Bob has continued to produce thirty to forty pieces a year.

◀ Construction workers eat a bacon-and-egg breakfast at Jay's Lunch Bar in Beaufort Street, Northbridge, before an arduous day on site.

▲ Year round, Kings Park provides an inspirational venue for walkers and runners — including John Burdett and Mia in midwinter. Its famed avenue of lemon-scented eucalypts was planted in September 1929 to mark the centenary of the colony.

▲ For Michael Chaney, Perth is the place to live. 'It's big enough to have everything you want and small enough to be manageable,' he says. 'Besides, in Perth you are not influenced so much by what others think.' He has retired as the chief executive officer of Western Australia's biggest home-grown corporation, Wesfarmers, and has a new job as chairman of the National Australia Bank. But he won't leave Perth. Notwithstanding the travel demands this will entail, he is hoping he can devote more time to his passion for furniture making. With the guidance of furniture designer Glen Holst of Bridgetown, he has built private workshops and he designs and crafts furniture from jarrah, sheoak, Huon pine and blackbutt. 'He's a skilled enthusiastic amateur,' says Glen. 'Mike's unique in that he goes straight to the professionals to improve his skills and he has a good eye for design — much the same way he operates in business.'

▶ Fiona Stanley is brimming with energy. A professor of pediatrics, biostatistician, author, champion of Aboriginal health issues, inspirational leader and Australian of the Year for 2004, she is also Director of the groundbreaking Telethon Institute for Child Health Research. 'I couldn't have achieved something like this in New York, London or Sydney,' she says. 'It's a case where isolation is actually empowering. What we had was a vision of what could be achieved if those of us from different fields of science — but with the same passions and interests — joined forces and worked together. It was pioneering stuff — a multidisciplinary approach under the one roof … the sort of bold idea you can have when you're starting from scratch.'

▲ It seems that West Australian native flora runs in Philippa Nikulinsky's veins. She is a natural history artist and illustrator who has published five books, most recently Life on the Rocks, and whose work appears in calendars and on prints and posters. Born in Kalgoorlie in 1942, Philippa is a former art teacher who has been featured in National Geographic for her illustrations. Philippa is pictured with the striking blossoms of silver princess (Eucalyptus caesia), found near granite outcrops on the plains east of Perth and often grown in suburban gardens.

▶ The curator of the Western Australian Museum since 1989, John Long has become an undercover agent in the fight against the illegal fossil trade. His pursuit of fossil thieves led to his co-authorship of The Dinosaur Dealers, along with an SBS-TV special alerting the world community to the problem of fossil theft. 'I'm just a palaeontologist who does museum things and writes children's books,' he says, 'but the press seems to pay more attention to the investigative stuff.' He has pursued the theft of fossilised dinosaur footprints from the Broome area in 1996 — the only fossilised evidence that stegosaurus once roamed the world. Unfortunately the search has so far proved fruitless. Among Dr Long's other achievements is outstanding work on the gogo fish fossils in the Kimberley which won him a Eureka Prize in 2001 for his promotion of science — and a starring role for the gogo fish as WA's fossil emblem.

▲ As a world-renowned blues guitarist, Dave Hole is an atypical example. He is quietly spoken, modest and a fitness fanatic — running eight kilometres every second day around the hills near his Darlington home. He has produced eight albums since 1990 and is the darling of the influential Guitar Player magazine. Born in Cheshire, England, in 1948, Dave came to Perth with his parents as a four-year-old. He took up guitar at the age of eleven, but soon discarded it. Then, at sixteen, he was reinspired and after twenty-five years of refining his art in the pubs and clubs of Perth, he sent his recordings to Guitar Player. He became an overnight success. Today he plays most often in the United States and is the only non-US artist on the famed Alligator blues label.

▸ Julie Dowling's search through her family's history and a desire to act as a translator between Aboriginal and European cultures, has given rise to some of the most collectible contemporary paintings in Australia. Julie (right) and her identical twin, Carol, have Aboriginal ancestry — their great-great-grandmother, Melbin, was one of the Yamatji people from the mid-west of Western Australia. Julie rose to prominence in 2000 when she won the Telstra Indigenous Art Award and then became the first Aboriginal female finalist in the prestigious Doug Moran Art Prize. Carol is a former broadcaster and university lecturer and is now documenting her family's oral history. Together, the sisters inform and inspire each other's work. The portrait on the left is of Mollie, their grandmother. Born in 1917, she was a conductress on Perth's trams, but had to disguise her Aboriginality because, at that time, Aborigines were subject to a curfew in Perth. The three men in the portrait on the right are Mollie's brothers.

▸ Antonio Battistessa fashions surrealistic sculpture out of iron as if it were modelling clay. His work is inspired by Gaudi, Dali and Toulouse-Lautrec and his studio in the Swan Valley is a treasure trove of discarded iron and timber waiting to become more of his breathtaking balustrades, benches or candelabras. While Antonio's creations seem like they are from another world, his heritage is firmly rooted in this world — the son of a northern Italian father and a southern Italian mother, his family was one of six to settle the Valley. He became an apprentice blacksmith at the Midland railway workshops when he was fifteen and after switching to driving road trains, he tried to make a living as a sculptor. In 1990, he succeeded. He has since produced outstanding works for Matilda Bay Restaurant, Lamont's Winery and Craftwood Artisan Gallery. Numerous pieces have also found their way into international collections.

◂ Shaun Tan, a full-time freelance illustrator since 1997, is often surprised by how his multi-award-winning work is received. The intricately crafted picture book is his specialty but he is frustrated by people's assumption that it is a medium only for young children. 'I am looking to awaken the child in everyone,' he says, 'regardless of age.' Here, Shaun works on a mural for Subiaco City Library — inspired by the room, its contents, Alice in Wonderland and a lot of 'unattached' ideas.

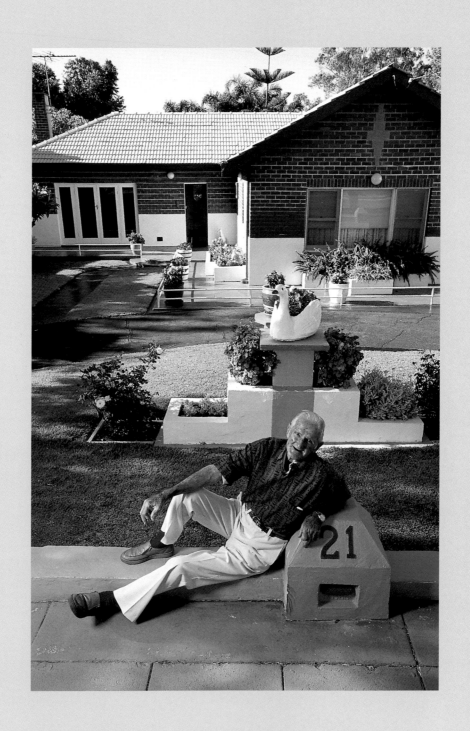

▲ As real estate, it is a four-bedroom, two-bathroom house with heritage listing and a guesthouse licence in craggily handsome East Fremantle — an elevated position within easy walking distance of the river and the port. To the visitor it is a breathtakingly bizarre collection of visual and tactile stimuli created by its owner, artist Andrew Hayim-de Vries. Screening his house from the street is the Wall of Life — adorned with myriad found objects held together by silicon glue. Behind the original front room-cum-studio are a railway carriage and a maze of other rooms, a sundeck, a tower and outdoor spaces with palms and ficus. Guests come from all over the world and pay five-star prices to stay among this cornucopia of kitcsh.

◀ 'I painted it these colours because I wanted something that no-one else had. I can assure you that I have ridden all over Claremont, Cottesloe and Nedlands and there's nothing like it!' Vic Shaylor finished building his house in 1960 at a cost of £2700 and reckons that nothing in Claremont Crescent, Swanbourne, would sell for less than $600,000 today. Before he built this house, he had lived in his parents' home next door. 'I love this house,' he says, 'you never know how long you've got at my age, but I'm not going anywhere. I'll die here.'

▲ Lawn bowls has been played in Perth's ideal conditions for 120 years, but the game has probably never seen as much change as in recent years. Once a game for retired people in stiff white uniforms, it now attracts many different people of all ages. The first club in Perth was formed in 1884, forty-three years after the first recorded game of bowls in Australia, at the back of a tavern in Hobart, Tasmania. Today, more than 13,000 people are active members of Perth's suburban bowling clubs.

▸ While butcher shops continue to disappear with the advance of the supermarket, father and son Bill and William McCreery believe there will always be a demand for their continental smallgoods. Their produce is prepared in their little shop in Middle Swan and the butchers know most of their customers by name, greeting them with good-humoured banter. 'Our customers are very fussy and we give a very personal service,' says William. 'We never prepackage meat, because customers want to know it is fresh and they can have it cut exactly how they want it.'

▲ Organisers were overwhelmed when more than sixty entrants turned up for the Face of Ascot competition on Oaks Day at Ascot Racecourse, but an appreciative crowd gave them a warm welcome to the catwalk. The winner was Holly Loxton, who walked away with a modelling engagement, a motor scooter and other prizes, while onlookers avoided the unexpected heat by standing in the marquees or under the trees. Many had come in extravagant hats and it was difficult to believe that some of them had been created just hours before.

▸ The first recorded horse race in Western Australia was on Cockburn beach in 1833; the sport of kings has been a feature of Perth life ever since. Established in 1852, the Western Australian Turf Club is the official industry body with its headquarters and principal course at Ascot, about ten kilometres from the city centre. The major event of the year is the 3200-metre Perth Cup which is held on New Year's Day for prize money of $350,000. Despite the invariably hot weather, the event attracts crowds of around 30,000. During the winter months, meetings are held at the Belmont Racecourse, a few bends down the Swan River towards the city.

▲ Tran's Emporium in Northbridge is as much about the diversity of Perth's cuisine as it is about the courage of the city's immigrants. Since opening its doors in 1997, Tran's has become a major importer, distributor, wholesaler and retailer of a vast array of Asian food. Tran Tan and his extended family of twenty escaped Vietnam in 1978. After an agonising wait in Malaysia, they migrated to Perth. In 1987 they opened the Emporium on Newcastle Street. Today, Tan's son, Trung, and Trung's wife, Moc Dzung, manage the store. Tan's daughter, Phuong Harris, pictured at left with her son Roger and husband Steven, also works in the Emporium. They are joined by customers Joseph and Anne Courtney.

◄ During the week Armando (Arnold) and Antonietta (Ann) Yozzi tend ten thousand orange and apple trees in the Chittering Valley, eighty kilometres away, and on weekends they sell their organic produce at the Fremantle Markets. Their brimming stall is also an outlet for produce from other growers in the Chittering Valley and elsewhere around Perth. Arnold and Ann set up their stall when the markets began their revival in 1975 and they have been there ever since. What has kept them going all this time? 'It's a way of life. We love to be in the orchard and then we love going to Fremantle on the weekend. Country, then city and then back to country,' says Armando. His father developed the forty-five-hectare property after migrating from Calabria, Italy, in the 1920s. 'I don't know how much longer we can keep going,' says Armando, 'I'm getting a bit long in the tooth.'

▶ Perth has a thriving Chinese community as a result of major immigration waves during the gold rushes of the late nineteenth century and during the 1970s. Chinese-Australians have had a major effect on many aspects of Western Australia's life, but perhaps their most obvious impact has been in cuisine. The drinking of tea (cha) is said to have originated with a camellia leaf in Emperor Shen Nung's boiling water 5000 years ago. Today, the tradition of yum cha — a meal built on tea with Cantonese delicacies such as dim sum, dumplings, spare ribs, chicken feet and prawns — is perpetuated in teahouses around the city. Seven-year-olds Michaela Anderson and Claire Shearwood eat their fill at Genting Palace, Burswood Resort.

◀ Eleni Kakulas spent her formative years working in Kakulas Bros store in Northbridge, established in 1929 by her grandfather and continued today by her father, his two brothers and two sisters. She enjoyed the experience so much that in 1994 she set up her own store in Fremantle — and as a humorous feminist riposte she called it Kakulas Sister Grocers. Housed in what used to be the entrance to the Princess May Theatre, its arches soar over a rich range of produce. People come to smell and touch, to experience the food and to discuss it with the staff of eight. 'I hope I can hand it over to my daughter one day,' says Eleni, 'or my son.'

▲ First came the llamas — out of a desire in 1988 to farm something. And from them came the theme for a whole new way of life for Wendy Fandry — accommodation, a function centre, entertainment, Latin dancing, llama tours led by Chilean Robinson Vivanco and the sale of llamas as pack animals. In the centre of it all is her family home, built in 1995 — a stunning reproduction of a 15th century French provincial adobe-style house featuring a bay window with a breathtaking view of the steep jarrah forest that surrounds the Southglen Estate near Glen Forrest. Upstairs there is another surprise, a flat earthen roof planted with lawn — complete with the telltale signs of invited llamas and straying kangaroos. And what is the special charm of llamas? 'They are such social animals, they are so friendly and docile — and like almost no other animal, you meet them at eye level,' says Wendy. You could even welcome them into your home.

▶ The international success of the Wheels & Doll Baby fashion label caused Melanie Greensmith to move from Sydney to Perth in 2000 in search of a quieter lifestyle. But fame has pursued her and partner Mark McEntee, a former guitarist with the rock band, The Divinyls. From their Tudor-style home on a six-hectare property, Melanie continues to design clothes for the likes of Kylie Minogue, Elle MacPherson, Deborah Harry, Darryl Hannah, Tracy Ullman, Liz Hurley, Michael Jackson, the Rolling Stones, Bob Dylan and INXS. Her creations have also been worn by Cameron Diaz in Charlie's Angels and Sarah Michelle Gellar in Buffy the Vampire Slayer. Mark has been independently successful, writing and performing the soundtrack for the first Buffy movie, amongst other projects. But he says the demands of the fashion label are taking over his life and he feels that, 'while I used to be a composer, now I'm more of a poser.' He has a critical role in the label's quality control, using what he calls the 'hornometer' to test the finished products. Pictured at a tea party at their property, Melanie and Mark were joined by the Arab pony Lucky and bitch Fifi L'amour.

▸ The highlight of Perth's Australia Day celebrations on 26 January is the spectacular Skyworks fireworks display. Since 1984, the city's biggest crowds have gathered on vantage points along the river to see the fireworks which are released from the Narrows Bridge, barges, boats and city rooftops. Assembled by a team of thirty-five pyrotechnicians, the half-hour display is generated by ten tonnes of fireworks in 16,800 individual shots and is accompanied by a broadcast soundtrack. A 175-metre 'waterfall' from the bridge competes with a vast array of aerial charges at the rate of thirty shots a second.

◂ Emmanuel Quintal, from Rockingham, is a first-generation Australian of Portuguese heritage who takes great pride and pleasure in Australia Day. He decided to enhance the national costume — a singlet and stubby shorts — with Aussie memorabilia, topped off by a hat that 'couldn't get broken or stolen' carved out of a watermelon. Strolling through the crowds on South Perth foreshore, he was stopped 'every five metres' by people wanting to chat or take his picture — 'especially Japanese tourists. I've been doing this for the past three years and next year I'll do something different,' the Murdoch University marketing graduate said. 'It's a bit of a laugh.'

▲ Twice a year, they contest an invariably fierce derby at Subiaco Oval — Perth's two Australian Football League clubs, the West Coast Eagles and the Fremantle Football Club, known as the Dockers. The matches between the cross-town rivals were once dominated by the Eagles, but after a violent clash in 2000, the results have become more even. Playing their first AFL game in 1987, the Eagles made the grand final in 1991 and won the premiership in 1992 and 1994. The Dockers played their first game in 1995 and have had a more difficult passage, waiting eight years to play a finals match. The two clubs have memberships exceeding thirty thousand.

▶ Australia and India join battle at the Western Australian Cricket Association Ground, better known as the WACA. The surface is regarded as one of the best in world cricket, with a pitch that favours fast bowling. Once home to a trotting track and an airfield, the ground first became a venue for cricket in 1894. Western Australia was admitted as a full member to the national cricket competition in 1956 and won its first Sheffield Shield in 1968. Since then, WA has been highly successful, providing many players to the Australian team including the legendary duo Dennis Lillee and Rod Marsh and current Test stars Justin Langer, Damien Martyn and Adam Gilchrist.

▲ Although still comprising less than one per cent of the West Australian population, Perth's Islamic community has grown steadily. The first Muslims arrived in the north of the state in the early ninteenth century, most of them fishermen and pearl divers from the Indonesian archipelago and the Malay peninsular. They were later joined by Afghan cameleers, until the infamous White Australia Policy of 1901 severely restricted entry. The policy came to an end in 1972 and the Muslim community began to grow again with the arrival of Turkish and Lebanese migrants. Since then, they have been joined by Muslims from all over the world. Perth's Imam is pictured at the central mosque in Northbridge. Built in 1905, the mosque's Middle Eastern architecture was extensively renovated in the late 1990s.

▶ Regarded as one of Australia's most innovative theatre companies, Black Swan Theatre has had a string of celebrated successes since it started in 1991. The company has achieved acclaim for West Australian writers and performers — touring internationally and nationally. The cast of Bran Nue Day is pictured with chairperson Janet Holmes à Court. 'I am immensely proud of what Black Swan has been able to produce, particularly as it has been achieved with minimal financial resources and without a dedicated home or theatre in which to perform,' says Janet.

theStreets

theStreets

Fremantle was the first staging post for the establishment of the Colony of Western Australia, but the administration was centred at Perth, twenty kilometres upriver. Today, Perth, the state's commercial hub, is dominated by high-rise concrete and glass modernist towers, while Fremantle retains its ornate Victorian and Edwardian architectural heritage.

Twin-city tension is given its loudest voice in the rivalry between the state's two Australian Football League clubs — the West Coast Eagles and the Fremantle Dockers. A 'divide' is also expressed in the distinction between living north or south of the river; in the hills or on the coast. But these petty rivalries simply add spice to the character and diversity that are to be found all across the metropolitan area. South Perth, Subiaco, Mount Lawley, Leederville, Claremont, Joondalup, Armadale, Rockingham and Midland were all established for different reasons and have evolved into very different communities. Nevertheless, most suburbs feature tree-lined streets, parks, schools and small-scale shopping precincts with cinemas, restaurants, cafes and professional suites. And then there are the mega-shopping centres that have mushroomed and multiplied over the past four decades, with major developments at Morley, Cannington, Booragoon, Karrinyup and Whitfords.

Perth has grown steadily with its population. The older suburbs, clustered around the city, are ringed by new developments. It is very much a city of the family-owned home on its own block of land, leading to a low population density of only 1700 people per square kilometre. But this low density comes at a cost. Urban sprawl has created a strain on resources and a transport system based on the private car, with its insatiable appetite for freeways, roads and parking space, and a corresponding competition for funding with public transport. In an attempt to address the private–public transport imbalance, the state government is making a major commitment to the southern expansion of the passenger rail system, which will service almost a quarter of the metropolitan population when it opens in 2006.

Perth's population is expected to increase by almost fifty per cent over the next twenty-five years. There may be some arresting of the sprawl, however, with a change in settlement patterns tending towards more urban-infill medium and high-density developments.

previous page, left Rising in the Avon Valley to the north-east, the Swan River passes the city doorstep and winds its way to Fremantle. Land in the foreground was reclaimed from the river in the 1960s to make way for the Narrows Bridge and freeway interchange. The old Swan Brewery building (on the river bank, right) was closed in the 1970s when production moved to new facilities at Canning Vale. For the Nyungar people, the land around the brewery is a sacred site, home of the Wagyl. Despite lengthy protests and strong community support for the demolition of the buildings and the institution of a public park, the restoration of the brewery buildings into apartments, offices and restaurants was completed in the 1990s.

previous page, right Since 1974, increasingly big crowds of runners have been attracted to the annual City to Surf Fun Run. Runners of all ages enter the charity race, including more than two hundred in the over-sixty age group. Starting in St George's Terrace in the CBD, the run winds its tortuous way through West Perth, Subiaco, Jolimont, Perry Lakes and City Beach, terminating on a football oval by the ocean.

◀ Completed in 1898, the Windsor Hotel in South Perth is an outstanding example of fastidiously maintained Federation architecture.

▲ Oxford Street, Leederville, is typical of the development in recent years of Perth's suburban café strips. It offers a range of cuisine from Italian to Chinese, Greek to Japanese, with the added drawcard of an art-house cinema. Much of the original construction in and around Oxford Street was undertaken in the 1890s and early 1900s. Very much a workers' suburb in those days, it is now highly sought after and increasingly expensive inner-city real estate. Toby Craig, Kelly Stein and Mikhaila Todd cross Oxford Street on a winter's night.

previous page *Perth city skyline at dusk.*

◀ *Seen from the forecourt of Central Park, Newspaper House at 123 St Georges Terrace was built during the Depression to bring the West Australian newspaper onto the same location as the now defunct Daily News. Newspaper House was completed in time for the centenary of the West Australian in 1932, its art deco façade in keeping with those of the WA Trustee Co and Royal Insurance building, to the right of the picture, and the since-demolished St George's House, to the left of the picture. The three buildings were designed as an ensemble by Talbot Hobbs, Smith & Forbes Architects, and Newspaper House won a commercial building design award in 1935. The buildings have a 1:1 ratio of height of façade to width of the street — a design principle their towering neighbours have abandoned.*

▶ *Today's quaint and immaculately detailed bank chamber is yesterday's thriving Palace Hotel, built in 1895 at the height of the goldrush in Kalgoorlie and Boulder. Much of Perth's Victorian architecture disappeared during the 1970s in a building frenzy driven by the Pilbara mineral boom. Urban conservationists waged a fierce battle to retain and restore The Palace, which now forms the base of the fifty-two-storey BankWest Tower. Completed in 1988, the tower was home to the Bond Corporation and, in the penthouse floors, the Bond family. In the aftermath of the collapse of the corporation, the building was bought to house Western Australia's regional bank. The bank in turn passed from state ownership to full ownership by the Bank of Scotland in 2003.*

◀ *Its flowing form and brilliant colour are in stark contrast to the QVI building behind. Charles Perry's steel sculpture, Conical Fugue, was fabricated in the United States, assembled in Perth and installed on the St Georges Terrace site. Designed by renowned Sydney architect Harry Seidler, the forty-three-level QVI building attracted much attention even before it was completed in 1991. Its original plans had ten more floors and with its elevated position, would have been taller than its rivals; but a glut of office space and a shortage of funds caused it to be truncated. And the name? QV stands for quo vadis, Latin for 'where are you going?', taken from the title of the pioneering Hollywood movie.*

▶ *Pedestrian ramp on the northern side of the QVI building.*

▲ The intersection of William and Hay streets, seen from Central Park, is a historically significant city intersection. The site is dominated by the Wesley Church (left), built in 1870 to a Victorian Academic Gothic style designed by Richard Roach Jewell. On the diagonally opposite corner is the newly restored Gledden Building, designed by Harold Boas and completed in 1938 for the University of Western Australia on land bequeathed by entrepreneur and philanthropist Robert Gledden. Perth's only art deco tower, it mirrors the town hall tower and together they define the extent of the Hay Street Mall. The Gledden Building incorporates decorative references to Aboriginal culture which, according to the Heritage Council, were 'innovative and challenging for the Perth community' at that time. Opposite is the former Economic Store and Walsh's store, another fine art deco example, built in 1922.

▶ Using teams of convict labourers, construction of the Perth Town Hall, on the corner of Barrack and Hay streets, began in 1867. It was officially opened on Foundation Day, 1 June 1870, resplendent in nearly 100,000 jarrah shingles, milled from the forest in what was to become Kings Park. In the 1990s, its overbearing neighbour, the R&I Bank, was demolished, and a refurbishment of the hall stripped away many of the incongruous latter day additions. The hall's elegant clock tower, graceful arches and chequered Flemish bond brickwork glow with restored beauty.

▲ Since the arrival of the first European settlers, Aboriginal people have struggled for recognition and equal rights. Each July, NAIDOC week is held to celebrate and promote a greater understanding of Indigenous people and their diverse cultures. The commemoration began in the mid-1950s with the National Aborigines' Day Observance Committee (NADOC) and the decision to follow Aboriginal pastor Sir Douglas Nicholls' recommendation to nominate the second Sunday in July as a day of remembrance for Aboriginal people and to celebrate Aboriginal heritage. In 1991, recognition of Torres Strait Islanders changed the acronym to NAIDOC. The events and celebrations held during National Aboriginal and Torres Strait Islander Week in Perth begin in Forrest Place with a lively opening ceremony.

▶ His Majesty's Theatre — the Maj — built in 1904, is part of Perth's Edwardian heritage. Ivan King, actor and heritage conservationist, was appointed curator of the Museum of the Performing Arts at the Maj in 1980. He has built a collection of 35,000 pieces dating from the earliest days of the colony to mementos of modern blockbusters such as Les Miserables, Cats and 42nd Street. Memorabilia from visits by Dame Nellie Melba, Katharine Hepburn and Sir Robert Helpmann take pride of place. Ivan bemoans the loss of much of Perth's architectural heritage and feels it is time that Perth 'looked and acted its age'.

▲ Australian citizenship presentations at Council House on Australia Day, January 26.

▸ Since its formation in 1911, the Royal Australian Navy has had a close association with Fremantle. The naval training centre HMAS Leeuwin was established at Bicton in 1960 and HMAS Stirling, Australia's biggest fleet base, with more than 2500 naval personnel, was commissioned on Garden Island in 1978. Fremantle has been a major port of call for operations during both world wars, the Korean War, the Malaya conflict, the Vietnam War and the Persian Gulf and Iraqi wars. On occasions such as Foundation Day, the sailors are out in force.

◄ *The scene of a fatal shooting in 1925, Government House ballroom has also seen many regal and vice-regal functions. Government House is the residence of the governor who is appointed by the Queen as her representative in Western Australia. The present building was completed in 1864 and replaced an earlier poor design that lasted barely twenty-five years. While the architectural style of the building itself is Gothic Revival, the ballroom is Classic Revival, designed by J M Grainger, father of distinguished composer and pianist Percy Grainger. Government House stands in over three hectares of meticulous gardens on St Georges Terrace overlooking the Swan River.*

▲ *With its commanding views of river, park and city, Parliament House is in an ideal position. The original limestone structure was built in 1904 in Federation Academic Classical style, and it faced west. In 1964, additions left the building two-faced. Cast in a stripped Classical style from Donnybrook sandstone, the extensions were oriented to the east, overlooking the burgeoning city centre. The lower chamber of the West Australia Parliament, the Legislative Assembly, was created in 1890 with thirty elected members; it now has fifty-seven. The upper house, the Legislative Council, was originally formed by fifteen members nominated by the governor; it now has thirty-four elected members. Women MPs were not permitted until 1920 — the first to be elected in any Australian parliament was Edith Cowan, when she won her seat in the West Australian Legislative Assembly in 1921.*

▲ Under the Burke Labor governments of the 1980s, Perth's suburban rail system experienced a revival. The Perth Central Station was modernised, expanded and covered. The diesel electric locomotives pulling aged carriages were replaced with quieter and cleaner electrified railcars. A northern line was built in stages, pushing its way thirty kilometres to the burgeoning City of Joondalup. Many Perth commuters, such avid users of private vehicles, became converts to rail travel. In a further show of confidence, another line is now being constructed — emerging from below ground in the city to snake its way south along the Kwinana Freeway to Mandurah.

▲ Edith Cowan University began as a teaching college in 1902. Today it has 23,000 students, three thousand of them from more than eighty countries. ECU offers over 330 courses in psychology, science, education, business, engineering and computer science, and hosts the WA Police Academy and the Western Australian Academy of Performing Arts. The university has three metropolitan campuses and a regional campus in Bunbury, two hundred kilometres south of Perth. The Joondalup campus boasts the radical architecture of this administration building (pictured), plus a multi-million-dollar recreation centre and microbrewery. Despite its high-tech appearance, it is not unusual to find kangaroos wandering in from the neighbouring bush.

▲ Members of the WA Ballet perform Munaldjali, by Stephen and David Page, at the Quarry Amphitheatre in City Beach. The spectacular amphitheatre, opened in 1986, was once an abandoned quarry.

▶ Young dancers from the Yirra Yaakin theatre company perform the Emu Dance to the sounds of a didgeridoo. Yirra Yaakin (Nyungar for 'stand tall') seeks to combine entertainment with leadership in social and political issues. Formed in 1993, the company hosts a range of artistic, educational and developmental projects across the state, such as youth arts residencies, dance workshops, performances at national festivals, plays by leading Aboriginal writers, mediation programs in schools, music recording and the formation of an Aboriginal choir.

◀ Ten-year-old Taylor Robson's grandfather, Tom Daffin, fought in the Middle East and Africa during Word War Two. Tom died when she was four, and now Taylor proudly wears his medals and joins the Anzac Day March in the city along with her father Warren Robson (left), who was an Army Reservist for thirty-three years, and his mates from the Armoured Corps Association. They are part of an assembly of veterans and their descendants who, together with active servicemen and women, form a procession of eight thousand through the city.

▶ In the darkness they walk through the parkland to stand silently near the memorial, side by side with tens of thousands of others in the world's biggest Anzac Day Dawn Service. As the first light appears on the horizon, there is not a sound except the occasional muffled cough. On 25 April each year the day begins for many Perth people in Kings Park. Anzac Day originally commemorated the loss of eight thousand Australian and New Zealander volunteer soldiers in a failed campaign at Gallipoli, Turkey in 1915, but the day of observance now encompasses all those who have served in international conflicts.

◄ *Rottnest Island, one of Western Australia's premier holiday resorts, has a dark history as a penal settlement for Aborigines. It is not surprising, therefore, that most of the original buildings around Thomson Bay were built with convict labour using local materials and under the direction of the head jailer. Henry Vincent was superintendent of the prison for over twenty years until his retirement in 1867. The dominant structure is the prison (the octagonal 'Quad'), built in 1864, which saw many inmates die from measles and influenza. Now it is a guest house. Today's hotel was also completed in 1864, as Governor Hampton's summer residence. What is now the Lodge Resort was built as a reformatory in 1880 for boys as young as eight.*

▸ *Anyone who has cycled around the river can join. No one is in charge. Each year a member is appointed to 'make' the shirts, but there are no accounts. This informal cycling group grew out of a fitness campaign by returning members of the 1980 America's Cup crew. Today up to 150 gather on Fremantle's café strip from 6.30 on a weekend morning to make a forty or seventy-kilometre journey. There are international competitors and tourists but most are ordinary men, and a few women, building their fitness and relishing a relaxing coffee amongst friends.*

◄ The original wetlands of Claisebrook Cove, East Perth, were desecrated and defiled by industry for decades. Recent restoration of the surrounding area has included a bold attempt to recreate the watercourse and lakes, and to enhance them with public art. Tony Jones' six-metre Standing Figure proudly holds a model yacht as its face is turned by the wind. Nearby, an abandoned fishing boat, which Tony found on East Perth's foreshore and restored, is now permanently 'moored' on the northern side of the Cove as the Sea Queen.

▶ With its sculptural form a yacht of glass, steel and copper, the tower of the Swan Bells stands in Barrack Square, watching over the daily departures and arrivals of the Rottnest Island and South Perth ferries. The controversial bell tower was built in 2000 during the last days of the conservative Coalition government of Richard Court but is becoming an increasingly popular landmark. It houses a gift from the British government of the bells from the church of St Martin-in-the-Fields in London, which rang for several great historic occasion, perhaps most notably to welcome the return of Captain James Cook from the voyage on which he claimed Australia for Britian in 1788.

▲ *Perth is the restaurant capital of Australia with an ideal climate for alfresco dining from spring to autumn. James Street in Northbridge is a bustling culinary mecca boasting Italian and Greek, Thai, Chinese, Indian, Vietnamese, Japanese and contemporary seafood restaurants.*

▲ Busker Tibor Dulanyi claims a repertoire of hundreds of pop, rock and country songs. Wong Yuchan is a visiting student from Hong Kong, preparing to complete upper school so he can gain entrance to one of Perth's five universities. This is Northbidge on any night of the week at any time of the year — a diverse urban village across the railway tracks from Perth's CBD.

◀ For fifteen years, George Cappa worked as an underground miner in Boulder and Kalgoorlie, and then he came to Perth looking for a job. He started work as a storeman at European Foods in Northbridge. In 1989 they put him in charge of the coffee. Each day, under his supervision, the equivalent of eight thousand cups passes through roasting, cracking, grinding and packaging, to appear in stores under Braziliano and other labels. The business is owned by the Re family — the four daughters of Giovanni Re, the pioneer of the Re Store, a Northbridge institution. George never tires of the heady aromas of the roasting beans. He says he's still learning, grappling with new varieties and new blends. He is a keen connoisseur of short blacks, long blacks and macchiatos, but has cut his daily intake of sixteen cups down to five.

▸ A gas-fired furnace at about 1200 degrees Celsius melts the gold ore. Once cooled, it weighs six kilograms and is worth $100,000. The gold is then returned to the furnace for the next demonstration. The Perth Mint, which refines gold and produces precious metal coins, is one of the most popular tourist attractions in Perth. It boasts the dazzling International Gold Bar exhibition — a collection from 320 countries — and the Golden Beauty nugget, one of the biggest in the world. Built from Cottesloe and Rottnest Island limestone, the Perth Mint, an outstanding example of Federation Romanesque architecture, opened in 1899 and remains one of the world's oldest operating mints.

▲ The view from the Fremantle Port Authority Building provides a wonderful vista of the West End. During the mining-led boom of the 1970s, Fremantle resisted the wrecker's ball that destroyed much of Perth's architectural heritage and it has reaped a rich cultural reward ever since. The Round House, built in 1830, is at the water's edge, on Fishing Boat Harbour. On the other side of the railway line, the Georgian-style Maritime Museum is the dominant structure in Cliff Street. Phillimore Street (with the bus exiting) has a fine collection of Victorian-style buildings among which are the P&O Building, the Old Fire Station, the Chamber of Commerce and Customs House. Mouat Street (in the foreground), too, has a rich array of original offices and warehouses.

▲ The Round House, Fremantle's oldest public building, was built in 1830 as a lockup and jailers' home. From 1849, when convicts first arrived in Fremantle, it became the first staging point for prisoners who were escorted to the prison at the other end of town. The Round House was taken over by the City of Fremantle in 1982 and is now a popular tourist site. One hundred years younger is this steam locomotive, G123, which now pulls the Wizard's Express train to Pinjarra. It is part of the Hotham Valley Railway, run for and by enthusiasts and providing tours around Perth and into country Western Australia.

▶ With spectacular views of Fremantle port and city, surrounding suburbs and the ocean beyond Rottnest and Garden Islands, the Central War Memorial makes an ideal picnic spot. For the children it has none of the overtones of war, but the memorial commands both the view and the respect of citizens aware of the loss of 59,330 Australian servicemen and women during World War One. Standing fourteen metres high and carved from Donnybrook stone quarried from the south of the state, the memorial was built in 1928.

The late afternoon sun lights up facades in Fremantle's west end.

▲ *Fremantle markets viewed from the Sail and Anchor Pub Brewery in the heart of the South Terrace cafe strip.*

▸ *The South Terrace cafe strip is less like a street and more like an outsized catwalk for parading all that is fascinating about Fremantle. The iconic eatery, Pizza Bella Roma, jostles for attention with a Dome coffee shop, Gino's Cafe and thirty-five other cafes and restaurants offering Italian, Vietnamese, Japanese, Scandinavian, Lebanese, Indian, English, Mexican, Burmese, vegetarian and contemporary Australian fare — not to mention the fast-food chains. For the hordes of visitors there are also choices of clubs and pubs such as The Clink, Metropolis, the Sail and Anchor and the Norfolk. There are buskers in the arcades, on the footpaths and in the performance space outside the Fremantle Markets. Those with tables on the footpaths or by the windows have the A-list seats from which to enjoy the constant parade of vehicles with booming sound systems and look-at-me drivers. For a break from the streetside frenzy, visitors can always slip into the New Edition Bookshop or any of the many clothing and souvenir shops.*

▲ A stilt walker at the Fremantle Festival, an annual celebration of the sights, sounds and tastes of the popular port city.

◀ The Blessing of the Fleet festival and procession in Fremantle has its origins in a European tradition that dates from the twelfth century. Molfetta, on the southern coast of Italy, was a base hospital for Christian crusaders wounded in the holy war in Palestine. The soldiers returning from the Holy Land believed that paintings they carried of the Madonna and Child had protected them on the battlefield. Centuries later, migrants from Molfetta brought the tradition to Fremantle with them, and in 1950 a statue of Madonna dei Martiri, crafted by Con Samson of Subiaco, was carried at the head of the procession marking the beginning of the annual fishing season. In 1954, a statue of the Madonna, presented by the people of Capo d'Orlando to their fellow Sicilians in Fremantle, was added. For the remainder of the year, the statues are housed in the Marian Chapel in the Basilica of St Patrick in Fremantle.

theLand

theLand

The city of Perth sprawls over a narrow coastal plain forty kilometres wide at most, between the Indian Ocean and the Darling Scarp, on the edge of a continent that is the oldest land mass on the planet. Cut obliquely by the Swan River, greater metropolitan Perth stretches north to Joondalup, south to Rockingham and east to the suburbs that extend over the Scarp.

The region long sustained the Nyungar people, but early European visitors were unimpressed by the seemingly hostile landscape. Botanical curiosities were the main reason for visits by European ships. In 1688, English explorer William Dampier collected specimens but described the land as 'barren and waterless'. Holland's Willem de Vlamingh's crew came ashore in 1697, but his men became ill after eating the fruit of the zamia palm.

Captain Stirling made glowing reports of the Swan River area that led to the establishment of the colony in 1829. The early days of the settlement were anything but easy, however. One of the first colonists, Eliza Shaw, is recorded as having said, 'The man who reported this land to be good deserves hanging ten times over.'

While the colonists learned much from the local Aborigines about edible roots, finding water and various methods of fishing, they made the mistaken assumption that the soil that nurtured such magnificent trees as the jarrah, the wandoo and the tuart would yield good crops.

The salvation of Perth was the opening of the Avon Valley to the north-east, where land was suitable for crops and grazing. Extensive clearing for agriculture led to serious land degradation however, for which current generations — in the country and the city — are paying.

Perth's early economy was sustained by agriculture, in particular wheat and sheep, and farming still plays a part in the prosperity of the state. Since the 1890s however, the growth of Perth has been fueled by the phenomenal success of the state's mining industry. From gold to nickel to iron ore, the land has yielded extraordinary riches. There is now a keener appreciation by Perth people of their city's unique flora and fauna, and there is a somewhat better balance between wealth creation and conservation. Since the mid-1990s, Western Australia has had the nation's fastest growing economy, averaging five per cent annually — nearly twice the national average. Perhaps 'the man who reported this land to be good' now deserves to be praised ten times over.

previous page, left In winter the Avon River is a raging torrent, and host to the longest whitewater racing event in the world — the Avon Descent. In summer, the river shrinks to a series of pools along the granite river bed and boulders. A major part of the Avon's catchment area is the Avon Valley National Park, with its jarrah forest and marri and wandoo woodlands. The park is a haven for more than a hundred bird species, all manner of reptiles, the chuditch (marsupial 'cat'), and macropods such as the euro and the grey kangaroo. Further downstream, the Avon joins the Swan River before flowing into the Indian Ocean.

previous page, right Growing in nutrient-deficient soil is no problem for this seemingly delicate little plant. One of the Drosera species, the sundew has sticky glands on its leaves with which it attracts, captures and digests insects, making use of a valuable food source. There are about a hundred species worldwide, and this is one of the five or six found near Perth, growing in swamps at the base of the Darling Scarp on the city's eastern margins.

◀ Lechenaultia biloba is one of the prettiest flowers of the jarrah forest. Often growing low to the ground, it looks like a carpet on the forest floor and has been used to great effect in cultivated gardens. The blue flowering plant is one of twenty members of the Lechenaultia family — seventeen of which are found only in Western Australia. Various species are found inland from Perth with flowers that range from white through to scarlet. The plant takes its name from the French naturalist Leschenault de la Tour, who visited Australia in 1802–03 — unfortunately, the English botanist, Robert Brown, misspelt his name and it has remained in plant taxonomy ever since.

▲ Most of Perth nestles comfortably on the Swan Coastal Plain, viewed here looking east from Bold Park near City Beach, with the Darling Scarp looming in the background. The Darling Scarp ranges from 300 to 400 metres high and is the western boundary of a vast continental plateau.

previous page The glass and metal of Kings Park's Federation Walkway make a dramatic contrast to the tuart and marri trees. And the view from the walkway above Mounts Bay Road and across the Swan River to the CBD and South Perth is something to behold. The Federation Walkway is the treetop section of a stunning 620-metre ramble through Kings Park from the roundabout through the Botanic Garden and on to the Beedawong amphitheatre near Roe Gardens. But to enjoy the elevated walkway, including the fifty-two-metre bridge, you will have to be there in the daytime — for safety reasons it is closed at night. The good news is — it's free.

▲ There are a thousand picnic spots in Perth's natural treasure, Kings Park. Within easy strolling distance of this site are commanding views of the Swan River and the city. At the peak of the park is the so-called DNA tower, a twin steel spiral stair construction that affords spectacular 360 degree views from the top. On Fraser Avenue are a restaurant, a kiosk, the city's principal war memorial and lookout points that draw the sightseer into the heart of the city.

▶ They look, feel and sound as if they are made of fine paper. And they last almost as long. There are nearly a thousand indigenous species of daisy in Australia, including this everlasting daisy which blooms in endless carpets of colour in the drier regions north and east of Perth from spring and into summer. Under cultivation in Kings Park Botanic Gardens, they achieve an even longer display. Here and in the wild they are a protected species, but if harvested legally, they can be dried for almost permanent flower arrangements by hanging in bunches upside-down in a dark, well ventilated place.

◀ Western Australia is renowned for its vast range of delicate orchids. The common donkey orchid, Diuris corymbosa, prefers sandy soils throughout Perth and neighbouring regions. Although widespread, it is small, and its vivid blossoms appear for only a short period in the spring.

▶ Anigozanthos manglesii, the red and green kangaroo paw, is Western Australia's floral emblem, but its spectacular blooms appear for only a few weeks during spring. It has been such a success as a cut flower in the local market and internationally that it is now also grown commercially in the USA, Israel and Japan. There are ten other species of kangaroo paw, unique to the south-west of Australia, and there are also many hybrids, mostly developed by tissue culture. In their natural habitat, kangaroo paw flowers are pollinated by birds.

◄ Bounded by car parks and the suburban railway line, and for many years a light industrial site, contaminated by lead and overlaid with concrete, Cityfarm is a dream come true for Rosanne Scott, her partner Thom and their legion of volunteers. With the indulgence of the East Perth Redevelopment Authority, and as a youth branch of the Men of the Trees, Rosanne co-founded the project in 1993 and since then it has touched the lives of many young people. Vegetables, herbs, fruit trees, ducks and chickens flourish in the shadow of the windmill beside buildings rescued from the wrecker's ball. Tonnes of mulch and compost have been piled on the concrete to make raised gardens beds in the hope that roots will do what jackhammers cannot. Rosanne and Thom are seeking to secure an extended lease on the property, but in the meantime they continue to provide a refreshing contrast in pace and space to the city around them — a rural oasis in an urban streetscape.

▲ Stately jarrah trees (Eucalyptus marginata), found in gravel soils around Perth, produce some of the finest hardwood in the world. In the early days of the colony, the timber was a major income earner, becoming much sought after as Swan River mahogany. Its rich red-brown tones and beautiful grain have been used to great effect in furniture and internal fittings, while structural grade jarrah has been employed all around the world for railway sleepers, house framing and paving blocks.

▲ He lives in an unassuming suburban house, on an unassuming suburban block, but, unlike most people, Brian Bush has given over his double garage to one hundred reptiles, including the tiger snake (Notechis ater occidentalis) he is holding here. Brian, a veteran snakeman and educator, is at pains to debunk the myths that perpetuate the dangerous reputation of Australian snakes. 'More people die each year in Australia from horse riding-related accidents than from snakebite. We don't go around hitting horses on the head with a shovel!' he says. His position is diametrically opposed to that of media stars who, he says, wildly exaggerate the dangers of snakes. He says that the toxicity standard for snake venom based on the number of mice it can kill is relevant to mice — not humans. In the last twenty-five years, only two people are thought to have died from snakebite in Perth, compared to West Africa which has at least 23,000 snakebite deaths each year.

▶ Bobtail skinks (Tiliqua rugosa) are common on the bush around Perth, and even in some suburban gardens. They are usually slow, noisy and ponderous, but can move quickly if threatened or excited. They rely greatly on bluff for defence — opening their mouths wide, showing their purple tongues and hissing. They have serrated bony gums and a firm bite, though it will rarely break skin. If given the opportunity, bobtails will feast on tomatoes and strawberries, but their usual diet is flowers, berries, succulent leaves, spiders, insects, snails, and carrion. Bobtails breed in spring, with the same pairs re-joining each year to produce usually two live young.

◀ Eve Taylor is a guide at the Yanchep National Park caves where the temperature is always nineteen degrees Celsius, regardless of the weather outside. She started in the caves on a 'work for the dole' program in 1994. Her interest blossomed and she became a dedicated speleologist. Eve was among a group of amateurs who discovered the fossilised remains of megafauna in caves on the Nullarbor Plain in 2002. Along with her partner and fellow caver, Paul Devine, she discovered the leg bones of an extinct giant marsupial lion. Altogether eight marsupial lions, a giant kangaroo and a giant wombat were discovered. 'Caving is just the best,' Eve says, 'you never know what to expect.'

▲ While maintaining their abseiling skills, State Emergency Service volunteers Todd and Julie Pender enjoy the magnificent scenery at Blackwall Reach on the Swan River at Mosman Park. The limestone cliffs overlook one of the deepest bends in the river and are an ideal training venue. The husband-and-wife police officers are members of the Armadale SES — Julie has been a volunteer since 1989 and Todd since 1993. They are among two thousand volunteers in the SES, and thirty thousand in six groups under the control of the Department of Fire and Emergency Services Authority — turning out to fight fires, rescue the lost and injured, and to provide relief from storm, flood and fire damage. Being a volunteer when your day job is policing would seem onerous. 'It's our pleasure to help,' says Julie, 'and we like to think that if ever the shoe were on the other foot, someone would come to our aid.'

◀ Perth Zoo is internationally renowned for its successful breeding programs for threatened exotic and native animal species. The zoo opened in 1898 with two lions, a tiger and six staff, and has been open every day since. Its nineteen hectares of gardens and simulated environments are now home to over 1500 animals representing more than 220 different species. The zoo's residents include four Asian elephants (Elephas maximus) of which Tricia, who arrived in 1963 as a six-year-old, is the matriarch. Tricia enjoys morning walks around the grounds with keeper Michael Cranley and the canvases she paints are a popular item in the zoo shop.

▲ They lounge in the shade at the end of the practice fairway and take no notice as even the best-hit balls trickle to a standstill around the putting green nearby. This extended family are permanent residents at the Vines Resort in the Swan Valley, along with the ducks and many other bird species that are attracted by the verdant fairways, water features and dense gardens. Like the rest of the fauna, the kangaroos (Macropus fulginosus) reserve the right to bound into the gardens of the nearby apartments and private homes or into the neighbouring banksia woodland, and to return at their leisure. The resort has won national awards for its accommodation and golfing facilities, and it is obvious that the kangaroos rate it too.

◄ Viticulturists discovered the rich loam of the Swan valley when the colony was established in 1829. The valley floor was divided into a patchwork of holdings, many shaped like ribbons to provide landholders access to the river. Today, despite stiff competition from Margaret River, in the state's south-west, it remains a flourishing wine producing and tourism region. There are over fifty commercial vineyards ranging from the dominant Houghton Wine Company, whose early reputation was built by legendary winemaker Jack Mann, to a host of small family holdings such as the tiny Talijancich winery with its famous red and white liqueurs.

▲ Darlington Estate Winery restaurant is as well known for storing its wines in French oak barrels as it is for contemporary-style Australian and European cuisine. Summers in the hills tend to be more severe than in the nearby Swan valley or on the coastal plain, but for nine months of the year it's hard to match the rugged beauty, the endless procession of bird and wildlife, and the scent of the forest.

▲ Geese patrol the vines at Lamont Winery in the Swan valley.

▸ She is less than a day old, and her underdeveloped eyesight prevents her straying more than a sniff from the sustenance of her mother. But in a day or two she will be full of confidence and stretching her spindly legs. Before her spring arrival, she caused her owner, Erika Schramm, a string of sleepless nights, but the emergence before dawn of this daughter of a Warmblood stallion was more than worth the wait. She will grow up in the shadows of the Darling Scarp, eventually learning the intricacies of dressage and showjumping.

the Water

the Water

Perth is dominated by water, in both its abundance and its scarcity. The city sits on the shore of the Indian Ocean, straddling the banks of the Swan River, but is plagued by drought and water shortages.

The Swan River was named by Willem de Vlamingh, who led a Dutch expedition there that came ashore and captured black swans in January 1697. To the Nyungar, it is Derbarl Yerrigan, created when water filled the winding track left by the Wagyl, a winged serpent and keeper of rivers, lakes and springs.

In colonial times, most of the land around the river was used for agriculture, but it slowly gave way to industrial and residential development as the population grew. Competition for river frontage led to the establishment of long, narrow blocks. During the Great Depression, the city's river foreshore was permanently altered when the government employed out-of-work men to wall the city river banks. The greatest changes, however, came later. In 1955 the Stephenson-Hepburn Plan established a blueprint for developing Perth into a modern city with a balance of residential development, open space, recreation and bushland connected by a freeway parallel to the coast. This plan realigned the city's axis from east–west, along the river, to north–south along the freeway system.

Perth is blessed with a string of long, clean beaches. In summer, their coarse, creamy-coloured sands and clear waters are Perth's favourite playground from early morning until the sea breeze sweeps in around mid-afternoon. Most children have learnt to swim by the time they've learnt to read. There are reefs and islands close to shore and coastal waters are relatively shallow as far as Rottnest Island, with moderate swell and surf conditions.

The dominant ocean flow off the west coast is the Leeuwin Current, which carries warm water southwards, producing ideal conditions for rock lobsters and prawns. Whales, once hunted almost to extinction, have returned to the waters off Perth, joining dolphins and a variety of other marine life, including the infamous shark.

The prime real estate of Perth overlooks the river or the ocean, but no home in the city is further than twenty kilometres from either. And, just to be sure, many homes have a backyard swimming pool — the highest incidence in the nation.

previous page, left Perth has a chain of swamps and lakes, habitat of Cygnus atratus. The striking black swan is Western Australia's faunal emblem.

previous page, right A mere 18,000 years ago, the West Australian coastline was twelve kilometres west of Rottnest Island. The last glacial period separated Rottnest from the mainland and flooded the island's lake area. The lakes cover about two hundred hectares and average a salt concentration of about four times that of sea water. From 1831 until 1950 Rottnest was the state's only producer of salt.

◄ The modest boatshed on the river opposite Tom Nattrass's home on Mounts Bay Road was originally bought for £5 by his grandparents in 1944. In 1971, the family gave the boatshed to the Sea Scouts and it was later taken over by Barry Kollman. Tom has restored it to the family, and restored it as a handsome and distinctive landmark.

▲ The indigenous Nyungar people knew the island as Wadjemup. In 1696, Dutch Captain Willem de Vlamingh called it rotte nest (rat's nest) due to his mistaken identification of the marsupial quokka. Now, about 500,000 visitors come to the island each year — many of them to swim in the clear waters of The Basin on the northern coast, east of Longreach Bay.

▲ *Yacht after yacht glides silently by in the golden light — silent, that is, but for the sound of laughter and wine glasses clinking. This is a summertime institution in Perth — the twilight sailing competition. As the city lights glow brighter, the yachts weave their way around the Swan River. Champagne, picnic hampers and sails are opened. There's no hurry. On most yachts, passengers vastly outnumber crew, and none but the most competitive spoil the evening with thoughts of victory.*

▲ They are equally at home on Perth water or on mountainous seas. Jon Sanders (left) made the first single-handed triple circumnavigation of the world, aboard the fifteen-metre Parry Endeavour from May 1986 to March 1988 — a total of 658 days. The yacht is now on display at the Fremantle Maritime Museum. His protégé, David Dicks (right) was the youngest person — then aged only eighteen — to single-handedly circumnavigate the world without stopping.

▶ Perth has the highest yacht ownership per capita of any Australian city. Its first yacht club, Royal Perth, was established in 1841 and is just a few kilometres from the city centre. It has pens for both power boats and sail boats and shares Matilda Bay with the University of Western Australia. The club sponsored the 1983 assault on the America's Cup led by businessman Alan Bond aboard the wing-keeled Australia II. They became the first foreign winners of the Cup, fiercely defended by the United States for 132 years.

overleaf On the hottest days of summer, there's no better place to be. Cottesloe is a haven for locals and tourists alike.

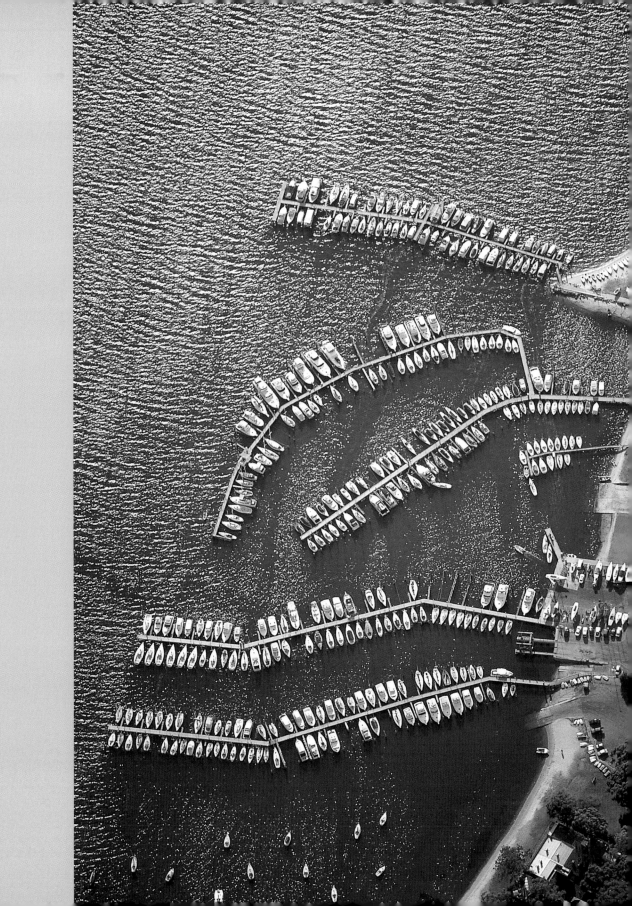

▲ The Swan River is the heart and soul of Perth. In the 175th year since the establishment of the city, the state government declared the Swan River as the first official heritage icon. Yet the river's popularity has brought with it overuse and degradation — it is a delicate environment that needs constant care. A program has been established to restore degraded river foreshores and wetlands and remove toxic algae from the Swan and the Canning rivers. One of the first projects has been restoring these wetlands at the Causeway.

▸ Most sensible people are still in bed, but once the rowing bug takes hold, rising at 4.30 am to be on the water at 5.30 becomes routine for the most unsensible of athletes, the dedicated rower. The city has a special charm at dawn and the rowers have the Swan River to themselves, but for the dolphins that occasionally cruise by. With only an oar, a tiny sliding seat, and the thinnest of shells keeping out the river, the rower is challenged not only to master the deceptively simple technique, but also to do it in unison with a team. Once it all comes together, it's heaven on water.

▲ Architects have made cunning use of afternoon light to create the illusion of the waters of Fremantle Harbour flowing into the WA Maritime Museum on Victoria Quay. The striking building is home to the winner of the 1983 America's Cup, Australia II, and Parry Endeavour, the fifteen-metre yacht that Jon Sanders sailed in his solo triple-circumnavigation of the globe in the mid-1980s. Visitors can also tour the shadowy form at the right, the submarine Ovens.

▶ The Royal Australian Navy's westernmost base is at Garden Island, connected by a groyne and bridge to the mainland at Rockingham. HMAS Stirling was opened in 1987 and is the home port for the Australian-built Collins class submarine. The subs play a critical role in intelligence gathering, surveillance and, if required, in anti-submarine warfare and maritime strike. Manned by a crew of only forty-five, the Collins class is seventy-eight metres long, has a displacement of 3350 tonnes submerged, can travel at over twenty knots underwater and dive to 180 metres.

▲ Fremantle is one of the US Navy's favoured rest and recreation destinations. American sailors enjoy the peaceful community, familiar culture, abundant shopping and romantic possibilities — and they provide a significant financial boost to the local economy. The USS Kitty Hawk (CV 63) is one such visitor, with more than 5000 sailors coming ashore while their vessel, America's oldest active warship, and the world's only permanently forward-deployed aircraft carrier, berths at Fremantle for several days. On this occasion, the Kitty Hawk was returning from Iraq, enroute to its home base in Yokosuka, Japan.

▶ The lighthouse on North Mole guides an incessant procession of shipping through Gage Roads into Fremantle Harbour. This may be the mariner's first landfall after a journey of thousands of nautical miles, but for the legion of fishermen who scramble over the rocks dumped a hundred years ago to form the entrance to the harbour, the 1906 lighthouse barely rates a mention. Their attention is on casting their lines into schools of herring, whiting, bream, flathead, tailor and skipjack. Jason Stein (right) and Brendan Oldham are among an estimated 640,000 West Australians who go fishing each year, making it the most popular pastime of all.

▲ Perth people have a love affair with the beach. But with every relationship comes responsibility. These under-12s at north Cottesloe spend Sunday mornings in summer with about 250 other youngsters learning the skills that save lives, instructed by volunteers who have graduated through the same under-age courses. Councils at all major metropolitan beaches run similar programs, as well as life saving competitions for adults. Clubs are funded through member subscriptions, corporate sponsorship and, in this case, by rental income from the famous Blue Duck Cafe above the North Cott clubrooms.

▶ For the diehard triathlete, even the worst of winter weather is not enough to halt training. Peter Randall, Paul Newsome, Warren Milward and Daniel Plews — members of the Challenge Stadium Triathlon Club — continue their open water practice undeterred. The club began taking members in 1990 and now has over 200 members. The triathletes also swim at the much warmer Challenge Stadium in Mt Claremont — venue of the World Swimming Championships in 1991 and 1997.

◀ Swimmers awaiting starters orders for the Rottnest Channel Swim.

▲ The nineteen-kilometre Rottnest Channel Swim, from Cottesloe beach to Rottnest Island, is an annual race that attracts over 2300 entrants. From dawn on a February morning, swimmers leave in staged groups for the longest ocean swim race in the world. Support teams wait in small craft and on surf paddles, seen here with the sail training ship Leeuwin. The fastest of the four-person teams and duos make the crossing in under four hours, while the best solo swimmers take just over that. The first recorded swim to Rottnest was from Fremantle by Gerd von Dincklage-Schulenburg in 1956 and took nearly ten hours.

◄ For someone to be called a 'galah', after Western Australia's ubiquitous pink and grey cockatoo, is derogatory, because it refers to the bird's erratic or stupid behaviour. But the pink and greys can be inspired. The small cockatoos are masters at finding water in the driest conditions, and in the middle of summer, a dripping shower head at City Beach is as good a source as any. Once found only in drier regions north and east of Perth, galahs are a common sight in the city. They often gather in raucous flocks, especially when preparing to roost at night, and it is not unusual to see them in light showers of rain, hanging upside down from power lines.

▲ Some paddle in the shallows and their voices travel along the shore, while others strike out for a three-kilometre return swim — but all love the friendship and support of the Port Beach Polar Bears. Their club membership is over a hundred, but at 5.15 am in the dead of winter, there may only be ten of the 'hard core'. After members struggled for years with thermos flasks in a corner of the ladies' changerooms, the Fremantle Surf Club allowed them to rent its old lookout tower and laid on the hot water. Now they have tea and toast after their swims and the walls are adorned with photos of the swim events and the social occasions that bring them together. These polar bears belong to one extended family.

◄ *Kyra Andrijich waits for the sea breeze to arrive at a sunbaked Cottesloe beach.*

▲ *A sunset procession of three hundred blue-painted people on Cottesloe beach marked the end of a recent Perth International Arts Festival. The ceremony featured fifty musicians playing an original work by local composer David Pye. The performers waded into the ocean while surf life savers and board surfers paddled out to sea to indicate the Indian Ocean theme of the next year's festival. The festival, established in 1953, attracts around 500,000 people to its mix of theatre, music, dance, visual arts and film.*

▲ Dogs and their owners have access to special exercise beaches along the Perth metropolitan coast. Canines of all breeds and dispositions enjoy a romp on the sand and in the water, but there is bound to be the occasional encounter that ends in tears.

▶ Late on a February afternoon, with the temperature still hovering around forty degrees Celsius, swimmers at Coogee, south of Fremantle, have a spectacular view of this storm approaching from the north-west.

◀ For most Perth beachgoers, swimming, picnicking and lying on the sand — or perhaps just being seen — constitute an active day at the beach. Despite the fact that the temperature frequently soars into the high thirties in Perth's summer, the beach is also the venue for more vigorous pastimes. For those wanting to remain on land, there is beach volleyball — it can be played casually by any number of participants, but formal competitions engage teams of two, four or six. On the water there are the paddlers — in canoes and kayaks and on surf skis — and the surfers — board, boogie and body — while the recent marriage of sail and board has seen sports created that are as much aerial as aquatic.

▶ Perth's beaches have seen the arrival in recent years of the kitesurfing craze — hanging from a stunt kite attached to a surfboard or wakeboard. The sport was introduced to Australia in 1997 by former defence serviceman and sculptor Ian Young. An experienced kitesurfer can take off from the water and be airborne for lengthy periods, as pictured here off Rottnest Island.

▲ The Alcoa alumina refinery in the southern industrial suburb of Kwinana has been a coastal landmark since 1963. The transnational company, with its Australian headquarters in the suburb of Booragoon, provides employment for 3700 people. From its three local refineries it produces over seven million tonnes of alumina a year — meeting fifteen per cent of world demand.

▶ Golden grain flows like water from the giant concrete cells into the holds of waiting ships. On Perth's industrial strip at Kwinana, one of the Co-operative Bulk Handling group's facilities receives and stores vast volumes of grain for shipment. The annual summer harvest, which is mostly wheat, comes by road and train from the 320,000 square kilometres of Western Australia's grainbelt. There is a high-tech storage and cleaning centre at Forrestfield, in Perth's east, and storage facilities at regional ports on the south and west coasts. On average, the West Australian harvest is ten million tonnes, although in recent years, records close to twenty million tonnes have been achieved. Western Australia is a grain-producing powerhouse, averaging nearly forty per cent of the nation's production. Ninety-five per cent of the West Australian harvest is exported to twenty countries.

▲ There is nothing nicer on a warm summer's night than eating fish and chips and feeling the sea breeze drifting off the ocean.

▶ Swimming with the dolphins at Rockingham is an opportunity few would pass up. Terry Howson came from Broome to start dolphin tours in Cockburn Sound in 1989. Now he and his business partner, Aaron Heath, manage a team of guides who set out in search of the dolphins seven days a week, nine months of the year. It's a well-oiled operation, with a heavy emphasis on safety, but there is such an enthusiasm among the crew, you would think that this is a rare occurrence. For the swimmers it is, and a memory to be treasured forever.

▲ The Duyfken bobs contentedly in the Swan River, serving as a tourist attraction as well as a life skills training vessel for young people from troubled and disadvantaged backgrounds. The square-rigger is a replica of the Dutch East India Company vessel the Duyfken, the first recorded European visitor to Western Australia in 1606.

▶ Six years after the project was conceived, the Endeavour replica was completed in Fremantle in 1993, made substantially from local jarrah timber. It has an overall length of thirty-three metres and a gross weight of nearly four hundred tonnes. Despite the different timber and a few modern concessions, it is an otherwise faithful replica of the converted coal vessel captained in 1768 by James Cook on his initial exploration of Australia. Cook was the first to accurately chart a substantial part of the eastern coastline and to fix the continent in navigational terms. Scientists on board collected thousands of plant and animal specimens that gave rise to major scientific discoveries. On his second visit in the Endeavour, in 1778, Cook proclaimed the east of the continent as a British colony.

▲ He spent the previous two summers building holiday homes for tourists in Croatia. But when the sun beats down in Perth, there's not much more you can do. Johnny Andrijich takes it easy the best way he can.

▶ The backyard swimming pool is as much a feature of suburban life as the barbecue. Though they are not all as stylish as Mark Barnaba's in Subiaco (featuring models Nicole and Joey) the backyard pool serves many a Perth family as a source of entertainment and a location for parties and casual meals throughout summer.

▲ The release of railway reserve overlooking Leighton beach in 1998 led to a titanic struggle for control between prospective developers, the government and conservationists. Leighton is a popular stretch of coastline between Cottesloe and Fremantle and has been dominated for decades by the railway marshalling yards and storage facilities. Protestors objected to the land being developed for high-density upmarket residential properties and campaigned for a revision of the planning guidelines to allow for dune restoration, open space and low cost-housing. After a vigorous campaign, and the sympathetic ear of a new Labor government, the protestors won a reprieve and the plan was redrawn. The new development features a reduced built component and more parks, open space and rehabilitated dunes.

▶ In her middle age, Shane Gould is still swimming times just outside her world best. As a fifteen-year-old, she won five individual medals at the 1972 Olympic Games in Munich — three gold, one silver and a bronze — and broke three world records. She retired a year later, having lost the joy of swimming. Shane moved to Margaret River, raised four children and took up surfing. Twenty-five years later her swimming interests were rekindled. She re-entered the pool and took part in distance events, including the 2001 Rottnest swim, but discovered faults in her swimming style. After some research, Shane found techniques which concentrated on flow and mastery in swimming, rather than competition, as a measure for success. She says, 'Rather than focusing totally on times and laps, having direct, playful, childlike experiences of being in the water can really improve enjoyment and speed. Two such experiences are finding balanced buoyancy, and an awareness of changing pressure and flows of the water over your skin.' Now a successful businesswoman, author and speaker on healthy living, Shane loves swimming again and is eager to teach her techniques to anyone who has a few hours to spare.